# Handel

## Study Guide

By Judy Wilcox

publishing

Elyria, OH

# Handel at the Court of Kings
## Study Guide

ISBN 10: 1-933573-04-X
ISBN 13: 978-1-933573-04-5
© 2006 by Zeezok Publishing

Published by:
Zeezok Publishing
PO Box 1960
Elyria, OH 44036

www.Zeezok.com
1-800-749-1681

# Map of the major cities Handel visited

## Handel's World and Place in Musical History

| | |
|---|---|
| Middle Ages | 450 – 1450 |
| Renaissance | 1450 – 1600 |
| **Baroque *(George F. Handel 1685 – 1759)*** | **1600 – 1750** |
| Classical | 1750 – 1820 |
| Romantic | 1820 – 1900 |
| 20th Century or New Music | 1900 – Present |

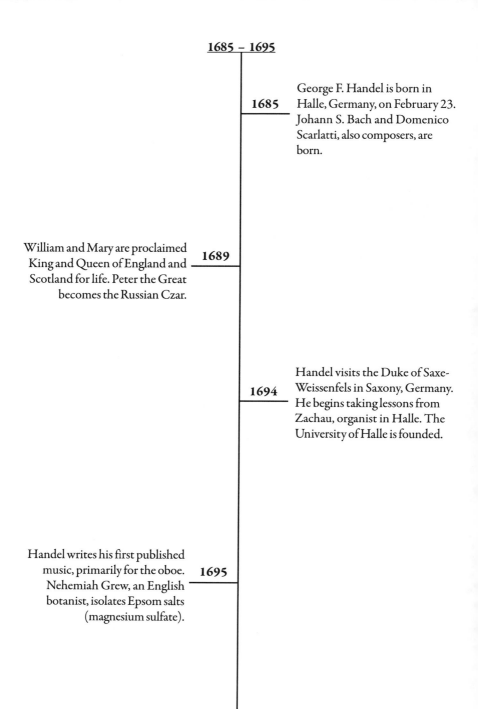

**1685 – 1695**

**1685** George F. Handel is born in Halle, Germany, on February 23. Johann S. Bach and Domenico Scarlatti, also composers, are born.

William and Mary are proclaimed King and Queen of England and Scotland for life. Peter the Great becomes the Russian Czar. **1689**

**1694** Handel visits the Duke of Saxe-Weissenfels in Saxony, Germany. He begins taking lessons from Zachau, organist in Halle. The University of Halle is founded.

Handel writes his first published music, primarily for the oboe. Nehemiah Grew, an English botanist, isolates Epsom salts (magnesium sulfate). **1695**

# Chapter One

**Reading Comprehension Questions**

1. At the start of this chapter, who was missing, according to the town crier?
   - George, Doctor Handel's son, p. 10.

2. When the "missing" George was found, where was he discovered?
   - George was in the streets, holding the torch for and singing with the wandering singers of Halle, pp. 11, 12.

3. Do you recall what occupation or job Dr. Handel wanted George to undertake?
   - He wanted George to become a lawyer — not a minstrel, pp. 13, 14.

4. Where did George and his aunt hide his birthday spinet so George could practice without angering his father?
   - In the attic, p. 19.

5. What did George do when his father refused to take him in the carriage to the Duke's palace at Saxe-Weissenfels?
   - George chased after the carriage on foot until noonday, pp. 25, 26.

6. What were some ways that George worked to improve his musical skills? (There are several possible answers here.)
   - He played his spinet during any spare moments (even during bedtime), p. 19. George listened to other musicians, pp. 14, 28, 30. He practiced until he mastered pieces, pp 23, 39. George copied compositions of German and Italian composers, p. 36. He also worked on his own compositions for various instruments, pp. 34, 36.

7.  Can you provide the name of at least one person who encouraged George's musical abilities?

• Aunt Anna took George to listen to the church chimes and hear the musicians in the market square, pp. 14, 15. She also surprised him with a spinet for his birthday, p. 18. George's teacher, Schoolmaster Praetorious, was another encourager by letting George play on the schoolmaster's spinet, and by loaning him music books, pp. 16, 18, 19. Herr Körner allowed George to play the organ at chapel, p. 31. George's new music teacher, Zachau, gave him lessons in harpsichord, organ, composition, violin, and oboe, p. 34.

## Character Qualities

*Focused (pp. 12, 14, 39)* – George was very attentive to music, whether it was finishing the melody with the minstrels (p. 12), going out early with his aunt to hear the town band at the market square (p. 14), or practicing a mass for church until he had it memorized (p. 39).

*Diligence (pp. 19, 23, 36, 38)* – George was diligent to improve his musical abilities by practicing during every spare moment (p. 19). He practiced until a piece was mastered (p. 23), and he spent hours copying master composers' works and writing his own pieces (p. 36). George also stayed late at church to practice for services (p. 38).

*Humility (pp. 16, 19, 26)* – Although George wanted to be a musician, he respected his father's wishes that he study to become a lawyer (p. 16). George was humble enough to practice in a cold, dark attic for the sake of music (p. 19). And he jogged a good portion of the way to the Duke's palace in his humble efforts to hear even more music (p. 26).

## Tidbits of Interest

*Page 9* – Halle is a town in the Saxony-Anhalt state of Germany, just northwest of Leipzig. Its name actually comes from a Celtic word for salt. The city is closely connected with salt production from the nearby marshes along the Saale river — an important tributary of the Elbe river. Salt was called "white gold" and was used as a form of money for purchasing items during the Middle Ages. In Handel's time, the rich salt deposits still remained a major source of income for the residents of the area (p. 35).

*Page 10* – Doctor Handel, also named George Handel, was a barber-surgeon for the Duke of Saxe-Weissenfels.[1] Doctor Handel was married twice and was thirty years older than his second wife, Dorothea Taust Handel. He was actually sixty-three years old when his son George was born. Dorothea was the daughter of a Lutheran pastor, and she was known as a good and pious woman.[2] Dorothea's sister, Anna Taust (Tante Anna), lived with the Handel family and nurtured the young George's musical interests.

*Page 12* – As Wheeler's story starts, George is six years old. Georg Friedrich or George Friderick Handel was born February 23, 1685. This was an important birth year for several musicians of note: Johann Sebastian Bach was born eighty miles southwest of Halle in Eisenach, Germany, just twenty-six days after Handel's arrival, and Domenico Scarlatti (Italy's premier harpsichord composer) was born in Naples, Italy, in October of 1685.

*Pages 12-14* – George's singing with the wandering minstrels mortified his father. Doctor Handel really wanted George to pursue an education in law, not in music. "[M]usicians at that period were regarded as a class of vagabonds, occupying a position even lower than that of servants. Most of the German servants, as Papa Handel pointed out, enjoyed the security of employment, while the vagabond musicians sang and starved their way over the gutters of Germany."[3]

*Page 14* – The market square where Tante Anna took George to hear the town band and the singers is looked over by four towers of the Liebfrauenkirche (the church where George later played the organ and took lessons from Zachau, p. 38). Immediately adjacent is the freestanding Rote Tower, or Red Tower, that soars 275 feet in the air. The Rote Tower has seventy-six bells chiming regularly throughout the day. Perhaps these are the chimes Tante Anna accompanied George to hear in the early mornings.

*Page 18* – Aunt Anna gave a spinet to George for his seventh birthday. A spinet is a small, compactly built harpsichord. Since a harpsichord's sound is achieved by the keystroke plucking the instrument's strings, by winding each string with cloth, the sound would have been muted (p. 19).

*Page 23* – The Duke of Saxe-Weissenfels was Johann Adolf I, successor to Duke Augustus of Saxony (for whom George's father was the surgeon-in-ordinary and once had been a chamber valet).[4] The cousin of George's who was the current valet to the Duke was also named George, George Christian Handel.

*Page 33* – Young George was only eight or nine when the Duke heard him play the church postlude and commanded Dr. Handel to encourage such talent in his son.

*Page 34* – When the Handels returned to Halle, George began taking lessons from Friedrich Wilhelm Zachau (sometimes spelled Zachow), who was the organist of Liebfrauenkirche (Church of Our

Lady) in Halle. By the way, Martin Luther once preached at this church.[5] George trained with Zachau for three years, and Zachau instilled in the young musician a lifelong intellectual curiosity. Zachau's method was practical (not just theoretical), and he required George to compose a complete motet or cantata each week, in addition to his regular exercises.[6]

*Pages 40, 41* – Zachau convinced Dr. Handel that George needed to go to the royal court in Berlin to learn from the musical masters there. In fact, George was always indebted to Zachau for his encouragement and instruction. George began sending the music teacher's widow frequent gifts of money to help her out after Zachau's death in 1712.

**1696 – 1703**

**1696**

George F. Handel is sent to Berlin to make an impression on the court. Peter the Great sends fifty young Russians to study shipbuilding and fortifications in Venice, Holland, and England.

Handel's father dies twelve days before George's twelfth birthday. The last remains of Mayan civilization are destroyed by the Spanish in Yucatan. The Court of Versailles becomes a model for European courts.

**1697**

**1701**

War of the Spanish Succession begins (and continues until 1714).

Handel enters the University of Halle as a law student.

**1702**

**1703**

Handel quits at the university and resigns from Domkirche to move to Hamburg. Peter the Great lays the foundations of St. Petersburg. Revivalists Jonathan Edwards and John Wesley are both born.

# *Chapter Two*

**Reading Comprehension Questions**

1. At the start of this chapter, to what city was George headed and why?
   - Berlin, for the Elector's Court, where he could hear the music of masters like Ariosti and Buononcini, p. 45.

2. What kind of contest arose at the Elector's court for which George readily volunteered?
   - A musical contest in which Ariosti would provide a theme, and George and Buononcini would then compose a piece from that theme, p. 48.

3. Why did George have to return rather suddenly to Halle?
   - George's father demanded it, p. 56. When he got home, George learned that his father was very ill, p. 57.

4. Can you list at least two ways in which George kept himself occupied in Halle when he returned home?
   - He continued attending Latin school, p. 59. He later began attending the University to study law, p. 60. George composed new songs, gave concerts, and continued playing for the church when Zachau was out of town, pp. 60, 66. He became the organist and choir director for the churches in Halle, pp. 60, 66.

5. At the end of this chapter, what evidence do we have that Mother Handel supported George's musical efforts and desires?
   - She gave George a small purse of money to help him get to Hamburg to study more music and make a living there, p. 67.

**Character Qualities**

*Undaunted (pp. 45, 48)* – George was not intimidated or frightened by the prospect of leaving his parents in order to get to Berlin (p. 45). He was eager to hear the music of the masters there. Moreover, he was not scared by Buononcini's musical challenge in the contest at the Court of the Elector (p. 48), though George would have been years younger than Buononcini.

*Leadership (pp. 57, 59, 66)* – George took the responsibility of earning a living for his mother, aunt, and two little sisters when Dr. Handel died (p. 57). George already demonstrated leadership in conducting musicians and singers even as a young man. He would compose new pieces and then strictly direct his classmates in the singing of those works (p. 59). He also directed music for seven churches in Halle, providing special compositions for each house of worship (p. 66).

*Hard-working (pp. 60, 62, 66)* – For a time, George provided income for his family after Dr. Handel's death *and* attended the University where he studied to become a lawyer (p. 60). He would get up before sunrise to work at the Cathedral where he had been hired as the choir director and organist (p. 62). Supplying music and direction for seven churches in Halle also demanded an incredible amount of effort and diligence (p. 66).

### Tidbits of Interest

*Page 45* – Help your children recognize that at this point in time Germany was made up of small states ruled by Electors who lived like royalty. During the Middle Ages, groups of princes were chosen to elect the emperor of the country, and these Electors had considerable power over their own courts or states. In 1696, when George went to visit Berlin, the Elector was Elector Friedrich III, who was trying to build a palace that rivaled Louis XIV's palace at Versailles in France. Elector Friedrich also wished Emperor Leopold I of Germany to coronate him as King of Prussia (a larger kingdom or state within Germany).[7] The coronation finally occurred in 1701.

*Pages 47, 48* – Buononcini and Ariosti were both Italian musicians befriended by the Elector's wife, Sophia Charlotte. There were some intriguing family ties among the acquaintances that George made in these youthful years. For example, Electress or Princess Charlotte was the daughter of the Elector of Hanover and the sister of Georg Ludwig, whom Handel later knew as King George I of England.[8] Princess Charlotte was a music lover who encouraged musicians within the royal court, and it is possible that her "encouragement" motivated the Elector to want to send Handel to study with the masters in Italy (p. 55).

*Pages 56, 57* – George had to return to Halle (a ten-day coach ride from Berlin) before his dreams of studying in Italy could be fulfilled. Shortly after his return to Halle, just twelve days before his twelfth birthday, George's father died.

*Page 60* – In addition to providing a small income for his family, George attended school at a new Latin school in Halle. In February of 1702, he registered as a student at Halle University, studying to become a lawyer. A month later (March 1702), Handel became the organist at the Calvinist Domkirche cathedral, which was somewhat ironic. He was a seventeen-year-old Lutheran receiving a salaried position at a Calvinist church. At the Domkirche (or Cathedral), George became "one of the foremost organists of the first half of the eighteenth century."[9] While he was there, George was responsible not only for performing on the organ, but also for caring for the organ and keeping it in perfect condition.

*Page 64* – In 1703 Handel quit the University, resigned from the Domkirche, and made plans to visit Hamburg, which was the cosmopolitan center of North German music at the time.

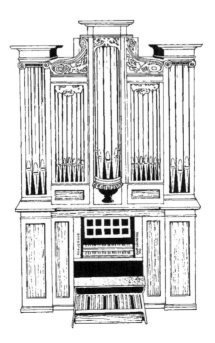

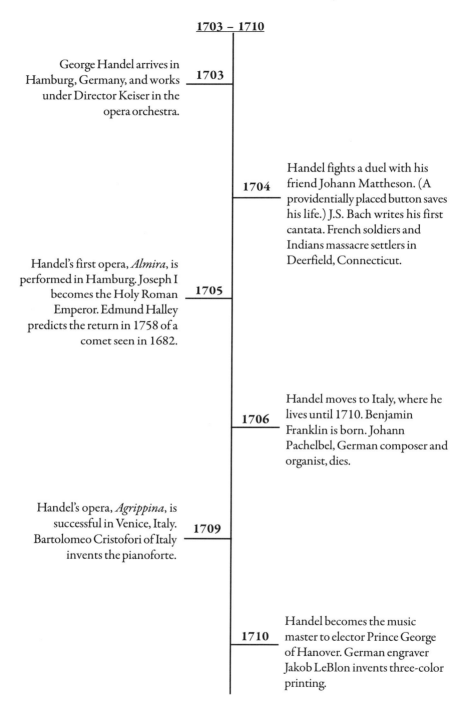

## 1703 – 1710

**1703** — George Handel arrives in Hamburg, Germany, and works under Director Keiser in the opera orchestra.

**1704** — Handel fights a duel with his friend Johann Mattheson. (A providentially placed button saves his life.) J.S. Bach writes his first cantata. French soldiers and Indians massacre settlers in Deerfield, Connecticut.

**1705** — Handel's first opera, *Almira*, is performed in Hamburg. Joseph I becomes the Holy Roman Emperor. Edmund Halley predicts the return in 1758 of a comet seen in 1682.

**1706** — Handel moves to Italy, where he lives until 1710. Benjamin Franklin is born. Johann Pachelbel, German composer and organist, dies.

**1709** — Handel's opera, *Agrippina*, is successful in Venice, Italy. Bartolomeo Cristofori of Italy invents the pianoforte.

**1710** — Handel becomes the music master to elector Prince George of Hanover. German engraver Jakob LeBlon invents three-color printing.

14

# *Chapter Three*

**Reading Comprehension Questions**

1. What was the first musical job George obtained when he arrived in Hamburg, and how did that position change in a single momentous day?

   • Handel became a violinist for an orchestra under Conductor Keiser at the opera house, p. 70. One day Handel directed the orchestra and musicians when Keiser was ill, p. 73. The directors of the opera house promptly offered Handel a position as leader for a year of the opera in Hamburg, p. 75.

2. George and Johann Mattheson, a fellow composer and singer in Hamburg, both tried for a specific musical position in the city of Lübeck. What was the job, and why did neither man end up taking the post?

   • The position was church organist at Marienkirche in Lübeck, a post the famous German organist Buxtehude was giving up because of his age. Neither man chose the post, however, because the arrangement required the new organist to marry Buxtehude's daughter, p. 82.

3. George met a couple of very important people from Italy — one while he was in Hamburg and one when he later moved to Venice. Do you recall who either of those men was?

   • George met Prince Medici while he was in Hamburg, p. 86, and later met the Italian composer Scarlatti when he lived in Venice, p. 93.

4. What was George's nickname when he was in Italy?

   • "The Saxon," p. 93.

5. At the end of this chapter, Handel agreed to take charge of the court music for which prince?

   • The Prince of Hanover, pp. 96, 97.

## Character Qualities

*Humor (pp. 72, 92, 93)* – George's sense of humor was evident in his practical joking in Director Keiser's orchestra. His teasing included: pretending to lose his place in the music, dropping his bow, and claiming the music was too difficult (p. 72). George also later hid behind a mask at a masquerade ball in Venice and teased the revelers with his musical talent (pp. 92, 93).

*Leadership (pp. 73-75)* – Handel did know when to stop joking, however, as he proved when he took leadership of the orchestra to rehearse them for the evening's opera (pp. 73, 74). His careful direction and initiative allowed the orchestra and singers to be perfectly prepared. Handel went on to direct the opera even better than Herr Keiser (p. 75).

*Respectful (p. 98)* – When he joined the Prince of Hanover's court, George acknowledged the Prince's leadership over him. When he wished to visit England, he requested a leave of absence from the Prince. He knew his proper place and the proper protocol in the Elector's court (p. 98).

## Tidbits of Interest

*Pages 69, 70* – Hamburg is described as a city of adventure and music. Hamburg is located right along the Elbe river as it opens to the North Sea, making it Germany's largest port city. Moreover, in Handel's time Hamburg was a city in which opera was being produced widely (combining French, Italian, and German styles). Remember, it was considered "the city" of music in northern Germany.

*Page 70* – Director Reinhard Keiser was the principal composer and manager of the theater and opera house in Hamburg. Keiser often tried to incorporate three or four different languages, fireworks, and elegant processions into his operas.[10] The leading tenor at the opera house was Johann Mattheson who was himself a composer and singer (p. 76). Handel became the second violinist in this opera's orchestra.

*Page 72* – Handel apparently enjoyed teasing others in a sober-faced manner. Mattheson stated, "He acted as though he could not count up to five...I know well how he will laugh up his sleeve when he reads this, though he laughs outwardly but little..."[11]

*Page 76* – Johann Mattheson was four years older than George.[12] He was a remarkable individual in his own right, able to play the organ, harp, bass, violin, flute, and oboe. He also studied law, sang in and wrote operas, and authored eighty-eight books on music, philosophy, and science.[13] It appears that the friendship between Mattheson and Handel may have grown beyond their association at the opera house in that Handel became a non-paying boarder at Mattheson's father's house in 1704. In addition, Mattheson would sing in operas composed and directed by Handel.

There is a side story of these two composers' relationship that reveals Handel as an adventurous musician. Once, when Handel refused to allow Mattheson to conduct a part of Mattheson's *own* opera, Mattheson became so angry that he boxed Handel's ears. They instantly drew their swords and began dueling, but Mattheson's weapon broke against a large button on Handel's coat (thankfully preventing the sword from going through Handel's body).[14] The button-and-broken-sword incident immediately released the tension from the situation, and their quarrel subsided nearly as rapidly as it had arisen.

*Page 81* – Lübeck is about forty miles from Hamburg. The famous organist Dietrich Buxtehude (pronounced \boox-teh-hoo-deh\) was

a Danish-German composer who remained the organist at Marienkirche (St. Mary's Church) for nearly forty years. To become the successor to Buxtehude would have been quite an honor, but the drawback to the position was that whoever inherited the post also "inherited" Buxtehude's unmarried, elderly daughter. Both Handel and Mattheson declined the offer. It's interesting to note that Johann Sebastian Bach turned down the same offer two years later.[15]

*Page 85* – Mattheson sang the lead part in George's first opera, *Almira*. Handel wrote and produced it just two years after arriving in Hamburg.

*Page 86* – It was during the opera off-season that Handel met Giovanni Gastone de´ Medici (pronounced \med-deh-chee\), the second surviving son of the Grand Duke of Tuscany, Italy. Handel accepted Prince Medici's invitation to visit Italy, where he ended up living from 1706 to 1710.

*Page 87* – Florence is known as Firenze in Italian and is in the northern-central portion of Italy's bootleg. The Medici family ruled Florence from 1434 to 1743. The family kept the peace and established rule in the region and also promoted art and culture in Florentine life. It is highly probable that Handel visited Prince Ferdinand, Giovanni Gastone's older brother, at the family palace. While visiting there, it is believed that Handel met Bartolomeo di Francesco Cristofori. For the Medici family, Cristofori built "several of the experimental instruments that were to lead him, by about 1711, to construct the *gravicembalo col piano e forte* that can reasonably be called the earliest piano."[16]

*Pages 92, 93* – Venice (known as Venezia in Italy) is a city built on over one hundred islets along the Adriatic Sea. Supported by millions of wooden stakes and canals linked together by some 400 bridges, it is the only city in the world built entirely on water. This certainly explains the need for riding in the unique Italian boat called a gondola (p. 91). During Carnival in Venice, a ten-day celebration before Lent, revelers and dancers experience a topsy-turvy life of giddiness, foolishness, and rebellion. Masks are worn by most partyers at Carnival to make everyone equal (ignoring class, gender, occupation, and so forth). While in Venice, Handel became known as "*Il Caro Sassone*," or "the dear Saxon." It was also during this time in the city of canals that Handel became good friends with Italy's foremost harpsichord composer, Domenico Scarlatti.[17] Yes, this is the same Scarlatti that shared George's birth year. It is said that Scarlatti's regard for Handel's musical virtuosity "became so intense that at a somewhat later period he never mentioned his rival in several contests of improvisation at the harpsichord and organ without crossing himself."[18]

*Pages 96, 97* – Handel's third opera, *Agrippina*, had been written in 1709 and was a success in Venice. Ernest Augustus of Hanover, brother of the Elector of Hanover, was so pleased by the opera that he urged Handel to visit Hanover in 1710.[19] Handel did visit and accepted Elector George Ludwig's invitation to become his director of court music. By the way, Hanover is the capital of the state of Lower Saxony in Germany.

*Page 98* – Handel obtained leave of the Elector to visit England, promising a quick return. He was actually absent from Hanover for almost exactly a year. He set foot on English soil in the autumn of 1710.[20]

## 1711 – 1759

**1711**
Handel's first London opera, *Rinaldo*, is completed in fourteen days and is performed in Queen's Hall. The clarinet is used for the first time in an orchestra. And English trumpeter John Shore invents the tuning fork.

**1713**
Peace Treaty of Utrecht ending War of the Spanish Succession is signed. Handel composes Utrecht *Te Deum* in honor of treaty's signing.

**1714**
Queen Anne dies and Elector George of Hanover becomes English monarch. D.G. Fahrenheit constructs mercury thermometer with temperature scale.

**1717**
Handel's *Water Music* is first given on the Thames. Future Empress Maria Theresa of Austria is born. Inoculation against smallpox is introduced in England by Lady Montagu.

**1718**
Handel acts as music mastor for the Duke of Chandos. William Penn dies. New Orleans is founded by the Mississippi Company.

**1719**
Handel returns to Germany briefly and misses visit with J.S. Bach by hours. Handel becomes director of London's Royal Academy of Music.

**1720**
Handel writes the Harpsichord Suite No. 5 with "The Harmonious Blacksmith." Spain occupies Texas. Wallpaper becomes fashionable in England.

**1723**
Handel purchases residence in London on Brook Street. Antony van Leeuwenhoek, Dutch scientist, credited with inventing the microscope, dies.

**1727**
Handel becomes a naturalized English citizen. George I dies, succeeded by son George II. Quakers demand abolition of slavery. Coffee is first planted in Brazil.

**1741**
Handel composes the *Messiah* in twenty-four days and visits Dublin, Ireland, for its first performance. (Some sources list 1742 as its first performance.) Maria Theresa accepts crown of Hungary, and future Emperor Joseph II is born. Antonio Vivaldi dies.

**1743**
*Messiah* first staged in London, England. Thomas Jefferson is born. French explorers reach the Rocky Mountains.

**1752**
Handel receives treatments on eyes from John Taylor. Ben Franklin invents lightning conductor. Great Britain adopts Gregorian calendar on September 14.

**1759**
Handel finishes series of ten concerts, dies on Good Friday, April 14, and is buried in Westminster Abbey.

# *Chapter Four*

**Reading Comprehension Questions**

1. The Queen of England asked Handel to write a special composition. What was this composition celebrating in England?
   • A new treaty England had signed, p. 107.

2. Why was Handel nervous about the Prince of Hanover's arrival in England?
   • Handel had been away from Hanover's court for so long, he feared the Prince would be angry with him, p. 108.

3. Why did Handel compose the work entitled *Water Music*?
   • He intended it to be played for the Prince/King while he floated down the river Thames on his way to a celebration of the King's coronation, p. 109.

4. Do you recall how Handel became inspired to compose "The Harmonious Blacksmith"?
   • During a thunderstorm, Handel sought shelter in a blacksmith's shop and listened to the blacksmith singing an old folk melody while he hammered on the anvil, p. 117.

5. What fellow German composer did Handel just miss meeting at his mother's home in Halle?
   • Johann Sebastian Bach, who had walked from Leipzig to meet Handel, p. 121.

6. What is perhaps Handel's most famous work — or at least his most famous oratorio? And where was it first performed?
   • *Messiah*, p. 123. It was performed first in Dublin, Ireland, p. 128.

7. What were audience members asked to do at the Music Hall in Dublin in order to make more room for additional guests?
   • The women were asked not to wear hoops under their dresses, and men were to come without swords, p. 128.

8. What physical struggle did Handel face as he grew older?
   • Blindness, p. 131.

9. Handel is known as one of the greatest composers and organists in the world. He is also known as the Father of the _____?
   • Oratorio, p. 133.

## Character Qualities

*Creativity (pp. 106, 109, 124)* – It required incredible creativity to compose an opera (*Rinaldo*) in only two weeks' time upon arriving in England (p. 106). Handel then went on to imagine soothing melodies that would serenade the new King aboard his barge on the Thames (p. 109). Finally, to compose a masterpiece like *Messiah* in only twenty-four days is nothing less than inspired (p. 124).

*Intentional (pp. 107, 109, 125-126, 131)* – Handel used his time deliberately — whether composing new works or training new singers while he was delayed from crossing the channel to Ireland (pp. 125, 126). He also composed certain pieces for specific purposes: to celebrate the treaty in England (p. 107), to appease the new King (p. 109), and to make its listeners better people, not merely to entertain the audience (p. 131).

*Generous (pp. 128, 130, 133)* – In spite of being away from England for a year, and in spite of some negative publicity about his works, Handel graciously agreed to come back to England to perform his oratorio *Messiah* (p. 128). Moreover, he conducted this famous composition for charitable causes such as the homeless children of the Foundling Hospital (p. 130). He also gave numerous concerts near the end of his life even though he was suffering from aging and blindness (p. 133). Only a generous heart could give so much physically *and* musically.

**Tidbits of Interest**

*Page 102* – In honor of the final supper Handel enjoyed at the inn near the North Sea, it seems only appropriate to serve sausages for supper while reading this chapter! There are several different types of sausage that can be readily found in most grocery stores, and that are fairly accurate ethnically to this story. These meats are often acquired tastes, but they will add some depth to your study by giving your children a flavor (truly) of German culture. You may wish to try any of the following sausage varieties:

• *Bratwurst* is a pale, smoked sausage made of finely minced veal, pork, ginger, nutmeg, and other spices.

• *Frankfurters* that are of the genuine German variety (which are *not* the same as American frankfurters) contain finely chopped lean pork with salted bacon fat, and are smoked.

• *Knockwurst* or *knackwurst*, which are short, plump smoked sausages that contain finely minced lean pork, beef, spices, and garlic, are often served with sauerkraut (another acquired taste).

• *Wienerwurst* is made of beef and pork flavored with coriander and garlic, and it is believed to be the origin of the American frankfurter. (Yes, even just a hot dog will do.)

*Page 106* – Handel was only twenty-five when he arrived in London, but his good reputation was well known in the musical world of that city. Aaron Hill, the director of the London Opera, for example, begged Handel for a new opera, and eleven days later that opera (*Rinaldo*) was ready for preliminary production.[21] It was performed at Queen's Theatre or Queen's Hall the day after Handel's twenty-sixth birthday, and it was called, "the first real operatic success in English history," which had been dominated by Italian opera up to that point.[22]

*Pages 107, 108* – The new treaty for which Queen Anne asked Handel to write a celebration composition was the Peace Treaty of Utrecht, ending the War of the Spanish Succession. The war had lasted over a decade (from 1701-1714) and was primarily a war over existing dominions and borders between Spain and France. England became involved in the conflict when France aggressively tried to enlarge its territories. Handel wrote the Utrecht *Te Deum* in honor of the treaty, and obtained royal permission to play it at St. Paul's Cathedral. (By the way, St. Paul's was the first cathedral in London built and dedicated to the Protestant faith.) Handel also wrote a "Birthday Ode" in honor of the Queen's birthday, which may explain why the Queen appointed him Official Composer of the British Court.[23]

The Queen died on August 1, 1714, shortly after promising Handel 200 pounds a year as the court's official composer. Elector George Ludwig of Hanover then became the monarch. It seems strange to think that a German elector would have any relationship with British royalty, but Elector George was a great-grandson of James I of England. This is the same King James I who had encouraged and participated in translating the Bible into English (the 1611 King James Version). Queen Anne had no heirs, so technically the next in line to attain the throne of England was Anne's half-brother James Francis Stuart, also known as the "Old Pretender." However, James was a Catholic and would not renounce Catholicism for the Church of England. This conflict between Anglican and Catholic religions created some strain in the country. There were even hints of potential revolts by Catholic supporters, primarily Scottish Jacobites, who wanted to place James Stuart on the throne by force. The nearest *Protestant* heir to the throne was Elector George Ludwig's mother, Sophia, but she was eighty years old and dying of an incurable disease. That situation propelled fifty-four-year-old George Ludwig as next in line to the throne.

King George I

*Pages 108, 109* – The Prince of Hanover was coming to London, then, to be crowned King of England. Because Handel had been away from Hanover longer than he had anticipated, he decided to write a special work to appease the new King while he sailed along the river Thames. The Thames is the main artery around which the city of London grew. By sailing its length, the new King could see and be seen by the residents of London. Ironically, while George Handel embraced English life and culture, King George Ludwig never really learned the English language and customs, preferring to leave England to its own devices, and choosing to live in Hanover as much as possible.

*Pages 110, 111* – The barges on which the royal court rode docked at Chelsea, which is a village outside the sprawl of central London. Handel's special composition, *Water Music*, was "superbly conceived for outdoor performance, and particularly for sounding over the wide, echoing spaces of a river."[24] The King was indeed pleased by the composition and pardoned his court composer for being away for so long.

*Pages 112-115* – After 1717, Handel began composing oratorios, which blend the "solemnity of the cantata with the lightness of the opera — a biblical drama in which the poem relates the story and the music supplies the scenery."[25]

*Page 116* – In addition to becoming an English citizen, Handel also Anglicized his name from Georg Friedrich to George Frederic. Handel stayed at the mansion of the Duke of Chandos from 1718 to 1720 and was master of the Duke's chapel along Edgeware Road.[26] The Duke had been the paymaster-general of the English armies during the War of the Spanish Succession.[27] He planned to build an elaborate palace that included a private road from his mansion to a nearby village called Cannons, nearly ten miles away.

*Page 117* – Perhaps Handel was exploring the new, private road up to Cannons when the thunderstorm let loose. Handel supposedly sought shelter at a smithy's shop in Whitchurch, which is another village closely connected to Cannons. A reporter in 1835 researched this story behind "Harmonious Blacksmith" and discovered an anvil at a forge near Whitchurch "that, when struck, gave out first a B and then an E, important notes in the key of E, in which *The Harmonious Blacksmith* is composed."[28]

*Page 120* – Handel returned to London, where he helped manage the Royal Academy of Music for the next seventeen years and invested his life savings in a new London opera house.[29] Handel even traveled to Dresden, Germany, in order to obtain singers for these operas. (Unfortunately for Handel, several unsuccessful opera seasons cost him his $50,000 of savings.[30])

*Page 121* – In October or November 1719, Handel revisited his mother's home in Halle, Germany. The *same* day Handel left Halle, Johann Sebastian Bach arrived from Leipzig (a good twenty-five mile walk) to meet the renowned musician. Bach was known as a man unafraid of long walks, but it is interesting that he never once left the country of Germany. One can only imagine what a meeting between these two master composers might have produced. Handel wanted his music to have an "overall strong effect on his listeners," while Bach focused on perfection in each of his compositions.[31] In either case, the power and impact of each of these German composers is undeniable.

*Page 122* – The individual who carefully copied Handel's works for printers was Johann Christoph Schmidt (later known as John Christopher Smith), who was a friend of Handel's from their days as schoolboys in Halle. Smith served as Handel's manager, treasurer, and general "go-fer" from 1717 to Handel's death.[32] Smith's son (also of the same name, but born in 1712) later served Handel long and faithfully as the composer's chief secretary — writing from dictation or copying an original manuscript — during Handel's blindness.[33] Both father and son served Handel for a period of nearly forty-two years, even living in his home in London on 57 Brook Street. Handel purchased the home in 1723, and it remained his residence until his death in 1759.

*Page 124* – Perhaps his greatest work was his oratorio *Messiah*, which he began composing on August 22, 1741, and completed on September 14, some twenty-four days later. That's 260 pages of manuscript filled in less than a month![34] Moreover, even though he was fifty-six when he finished *Messiah*, Handel announced that he was not tired and immediately began composing another biblical oratorio entitled *Samson*. Remarkably, Handel placed *Messiah* in a drawer where it was ignored for almost a year.

As a side note, Handel's use of biblical themes for his oratorios was often misunderstood by church people because the productions were performed in theaters — a revolutionary use of theater and a revolutionary way of presenting religious messages.[35] For example, among those who spoke out against theatrical performances of *Messiah* was John Newton, composer of "Amazing Grace."[36] Yet, Handel refused to respond to such attacks, and apparently had good relations with other church "pillars" like Charles Wesley, for whom he supplied the music for the hymn "Rejoice, the Lord is King."[37]

*Page 125* – The Lord-Lieutenant of Ireland was William Cavendish, the Duke of Devonshire. This invitation from Dublin restored Handel's spirits, which had been deflated by financial failures, jealous contemporaries, piracy of his works, and poor health.[38]

*Page 126* – Chester is a city northwest of London, near Liverpool. The Golden Falcon was an inn in Chester where Handel stayed during the storms that were preventing passage across the channel. The story of the singer who could sight-read music — but not on *first* sight — was recorded by Dr. Charles Burney, England's foremost musicologist, who was then a fifteen-year-old observer at the inn.[39] Handel went from Chester across the Irish Sea to Dublin, Ireland.

*Page 127* – Handel finally arrived in Ireland on November 18, 1741, when the storms subsided. The proceeds of the first production of *Messiah* went to three charitable undertakings, including a debtor's prison and the Foundling Hospital, and after that introductory performance anytime *Messiah* was presented, almost all the proceeds went to benefit charities.[40] While Handel never married or had a family of his own, he was always known as a charitable man who generously cared for widows and orphans.

*Page 128* – Fishamble Street was a market or "fish shambles" from the medieval period. The Charitable Music Society's Hall, where *Messiah* was performed, asked women to eliminate the hoops from under their dresses, and the men to leave their swords at home, and it is believed that the managers of the Hall increased the capacity from the usual six hundred persons to seven hundred by making such a request.[41] In 1743, Handel returned to England and staged *Messiah* in London.

Handel was known as rather temperamental, but even in his "most dramatic fits of agitation there was no real malice."[42] The mention of his trembling wig (p. 129) hints at his temperamental nature and at the continuing tension and controversy that surrounded Handel in England at the time. It also supports the idea that Handel was a large man who enjoyed wearing an oversized white wig with curls coming over the shoulder.[43]

*Page 129* – Following royal protocol, the entire audience at the *Messiah* presentation stood to their feet when the King rose, and this initiated the tradition of standing during the "Hallelujah Chorus" — a tradition that has lasted for more than two centuries.

*Pages 130, 131* – Lord George Henry Kinnoul praised *Messiah* as "fine entertainment," to which Handel replied in exasperation, "My lord, I should be sorry if I only entertained them; I wished to make them better."[44] As one biographer records, "It was Handel's ambition to make men think instead of relieving them from thinking."[45]

*Pages 131, 132* – In 1751, during the composing of a chorus for his newest oratorio, *Jephtha*, Handel stopped and noted at the bottom of the page that he was experiencing a relaxation of the sight in his left eye.[46] By 1752, as Handel entered his mid-sixties, his eyesight was weakened enough that he sought treatment from John Taylor, an "opthalmiater" who some call a quack doctor. Taylor had operated unsuccessfully on Bach's eyes just two years before, yet Handel was determined to be able to continue composing, and he needed his sight to do that well.[47] By the end of writing *Jephtha*, he could hardly see the notes with a magnifying glass. While Handel said he didn't fear darkness, he dreaded ending his work, so he endured painful treatments on the apparent cataracts in his eyes. According to reports, these treatments were done without anesthesia and consisted of "piercing the balls of his eyes with a needle."[48]

By the way, the Thomas Morrell mentioned in this chapter was a friend and pastor with whom Handel worked on at least three of his oratorios.

*Page 133* – Handel's impending blindness curtailed some of his composing abilities in the last years of his life, but he still sought music and his faith for comfort and encouragement. He would practice the harpsichord for hours each day, and then he organized performances to share that music with the public. He also continued regularly in his church worship at St. George's in Hanover Square in London.[49]

*Page 134* – In the spring of 1759, Handel organized a series of ten concerts that he would conduct, ending with the *Messiah* shortly before Easter. He had expressed to his friends a desire to die on Good Friday, "in the hope of rejoining the good God, my sweet Lord and Savior, on the day of His resurrection."[50] Only eight days after his final conducting of *Messiah*, and on Good Friday, April 14, he said farewell to his friends and asked his servant to leave him. "I have now done with the world,"[51] he said, and with that "the singer and his Messiah met face to face."[52]

Over three thousand people attended Handel's funeral, and he was honored by the royal court when he was buried in Poet's Corner in Westminster Abbey. A monument of George F. Handel in Westminster Abbey shows the "Father of the Oratorio" holding a manuscript for the solo start of *Messiah*'s third part, appropriately entitled "I know that my Redeemer liveth." Handel was honored to serve most of his life at the court of kings — but how much more glorious to be serving now in the Court of the King of Kings!

# *Endnotes*

[1] Herbert Weinstock, *Handel* (New York: Alfred A. Knopf, 1959), 7.

[2] Jane Stuart Smith and Betty Carlson, *The Gift of Music: Great Composers and Their Influence* (Wheaton, IL: Crossway Books, 1995), 39.

[3] Henry Thomas and Dana Lee Thomas, *Living Biographies of Great Composers* (Garden City, NY: Nelson Doubleday, Inc., 1940), 19.

[4] Weinstock, *Handel*, 7.

[5] Ibid., 11.

[6] Thomas and Thomas, *Living Biographies of Great Composers*, 21.

[7] Weinstock, *Handel*, 13.

[8] Ibid., 14.

[9] Ibid., 17.

[10] Louis Elson, *Great Composers and Their Work* (Boston: L.C. Page and Company, 1898), 59.

[11] Weinstock, *Handel*, 21.

[12] Elson, *Great Composers and Their Work*, 58.

[13] Thomas and Thomas, *Living Biographies of Great Composers*, 22.

[14] Elson, *Great Composers and Their Work*, 60.

[15] Thomas and Thomas, *Living Biographies of Great Composers*, 23.

[16] Weinstock, *Handel*, 29.

[17] Smith and Carlson, *The Gift of Music*, 40.

[18] Weinstock, *Handel*, 32.

[19] Ibid., 43.

[20] Ibid., 45.

[21] Thomas and Thomas, *Living Biographies of Great Composers*, 23.

[22] Weinstock, *Handel*, 56.

[23] Thomas and Thomas, *Living Biographies of Great Composers*, 28.

[24] Weinstock, *Handel*, 77.

[25] Thomas and Thomas, *Living Biographies of Great Composers*, 29.

[26] Smith and Carlson, *The Gift of Music*, 42.

[27] Weinstock, *Handel*, 83.

[28] Ibid., 86.

[29] Smith and Carlson, *The Gift of Music*, 42.

[30] Thomas and Thomas, *Living Biographies of Great Composers*, 30.

[31] Smith and Carlson, *The Gift of Music*, 41.

[32] Weinstock, *Handel*, 81.

[33] Ibid.

[34] Patrick Kavanaugh, *Spiritual Lives of the Great Composers* (Grand Rapids, MI: Zondervan, 1996), 30.

[35] Smith and Carlson, *The Gift of Music*, 43.

[36] Kavanaugh, *Spiritual Lives of the Great Composers*, 33.

[37] Smith and Carlson, *The Gift of Music*, 44.

[38] Thomas and Thomas, *Living Biographies of Great Composers*, 31.
[39] Weinstock, *Handel,* 233.
[40] Smith and Carlson, *The Gift of Music*, 45.
[41] Weinstock, *Handel*, 240.
[42] Smith and Carlson, *The Gift of Music*, 42.
[43] Ibid.
[44] Weinstock, *Handel*, 252.
[45] Thomas and Thomas, *Living Biographies of Great Composers*, 30.
[46] Smith and Carlson, *The Gift of Music*, 45.
[47] Weinstock, *Handel*, 294.
[48] Ibid.
[49] Smith and Carlson, *The Gift of Music*, 45.
[50] Ibid.
[51] Ibid.
[52] Thomas and Thomas, *Living Biographies of Great Composers*, 33.

# *Glossary of Musical Terms*

*Bourrée* – An old French dance resembling the gavotte, usually in quick double time beginning with an upbeat.

*Chaconne* – A kind of dance in a slow 3/4 time that first emerged in the 16th century.

*Courante* – A 17th-century French dance characterized by running and gliding steps to an accompaniment in triple time.

*Fugue* – A fugue begins with its subject (a brief musical theme) stated by one of the voices playing alone. A second voice then enters and plays the subject, while the first voice continues on with a contrapuntal accompaniment. Then the remaining voices similarly enter, one by one. The remainder of the fugue further develops the material using all of the voices.

*Fughetta* – A small fugue.

*Gavotte* – A French folk dance that takes its name from the Gavot people of the Pays de Gap region of Dauphiné, where the dance originated. It is in 4/4 or 2/2 time and is of moderate tempo.

*Hornpipe* – An English baroque dance in a lively 3/2 time.

*Intermezzo* – An instrumental piece which was either a movement between two other pieces of music in a larger work or a short independent instrumental composition.

*Largo* – Means the music is to be played at a slow tempo.

*Minuet* – A triple-meter (three beats per measure) French dance that was popular from the mid-17th century to the end of the 18th century.

*Passepied* – A spirited dance in triple meter, popular in France and England in the 17th and 18th centuries, resembling a minuet but faster.

*Prelude* – A short composition of the 15th and early 16th centuries written in a free style, usually for keyboard.

*Sonatina* – A little sonata; simpler in structure and shorter in length than a sonata.

*Vivace* – An Italian musical term indicating a movement that is in a lively mood (and so usually in a fast tempo).